How the Arabs Invented Algebra

The History of the Concept of Variables

Tika Downey

PowerMath™

The Rosen Publishing Group's
PowerKids Press™
New York

Published in 2004 by The Rosen Publishing Group, Inc.
29 East 21st Street, New York, NY 10010

Book Design: Haley Wilson

Photo Credits: Cover © Nevada Wier/Image Bank; pp. 4–32 (background) © Corbis; p. 5 © John Henley/Corbis; p. 9 © Archivo Iconografico, S. A./Corbis; p. 15 © Corbis; pp. 17, 19, 25 © Bettmann/Corbis; p. 21 © Richard Bickel/Corbis; p. 23 © Jonathan Blair/Corbis; p. 27 © David H. Wells/Corbis; p. 29 © David Turnley/Corbis.

Downey, Tika
How the Arabs invented algebra : the history of the
concept of variables / Tika Downey.
        p. cm. — (Powermath)
Includes index.
        Contents: Just what is algebra good for anyway? -- Ancient
        Baghdad — The house of wisdom — Al-khwarizmi invents algebra --
        Later Arab and Muslim mathematicians — Algebra finally reaches
        Europe — Math for merchants.
  ISBN 0-8239-8986-0 (lib.)
  ISBN 0-8239-8879-1 (pbk.)
  6-pack ISBN: 0-8239-7388-3
1. Mathematics, Arab—Juvenile literature   2. Algebra—
History—Juvenile literature   [1. Algebra—History]
I. Title   II. Series
QA27.A67.D68 2004   2003-003592
512—dc21

Contents

Just What Is Algebra Good for Anyway?

Algebra is a type of math that helps us solve certain types of problems more quickly and easily. Algebra problems have numbers like regular math problems, but they also have letters called **variables**. Variables stand for unknown numbers whose values you want to find. The numbers in algebra problems are called **constants**. Unlike the variables—whose value can change, or vary—the values of the numbers never change. For example, 5 is always 5. It never represents 7 or 12 or any other number. Let's look at a simple algebra **equation**.

$$x \text{ (variable)} + 10 \text{ (constant)} = 13 \text{ (constant)}$$
$$x = 3$$

In this example, it's easy to guess that $x = 3$, since you know that 13 is 3 more than 10. Even more difficult algebra problems are not too hard to solve.

Algebra was invented to help people solve problems that they had to deal with every day.

Let's look at a real-life situation where you can use algebra. Suppose that you and your friend Jill collected books to give to the library. You take your books to the library together. You collected 12 books. Altogether, you and Jill collected 27 books. How many books did Jill collect?

$$x \text{ (Jill's books)} + 12 \text{ (your books)} = 27 \text{ (total number of books)}$$

To find the value of x, you need to change the form of the equation so that x is alone on the left side. Then whatever you have on the right side will be the value of x.

You can get x alone by subtracting 12 from the left side of the equation. When you subtract 12 from the left side, you must also subtract 12 from the right side to keep both sides of the equation equal.

$$x + 12 = 27$$
$$x + 12 - 12 = 27 - 12$$
$$x = 15$$

You may wonder who first came up with this math we call algebra. It was invented in the ancient city of Baghdad almost 1,200 years ago!

27

12

Jill's books   **your books**   **total books**

When you solve an algebra problem, remember that you're dealing with an equation. The left side must always equal the right side. If you subtract 12 from the left side, you must also subtract 12 from the right side.

Ancient Baghdad

Today, Baghdad is the capital of Iraq. In 830 A.D., Baghdad was the capital of the vast Arabic-**Islamic** empire and an important trade center where people from many lands bought and sold goods. More than 2 million people lived in the city. Beautiful parks, gardens, and broad avenues filled the city. The people of Baghdad shopped at the city's many outdoor markets, where they bought food, dishes, cooking pots, cloth, and almost anything else they wanted. The Tigris (TYE-gruhs) River ran through the middle of the city, supplying plenty of clean water to the people who lived there.

Al-Mamun (al–mah-MOON), the ruler of the empire, lived in Baghdad in a huge marble palace that had its own private gardens and zoo. There was also a huge park filled with wild animals for al-Mamun and his friends to hunt. The palace gardens, zoo, and hunting park covered an area so large that it took hours to walk all the way around it!

This painting comes from a book written in the 1500s and shows a scene at the palace of Mirhah. Al-Mamun's palace probably looked much like this one.

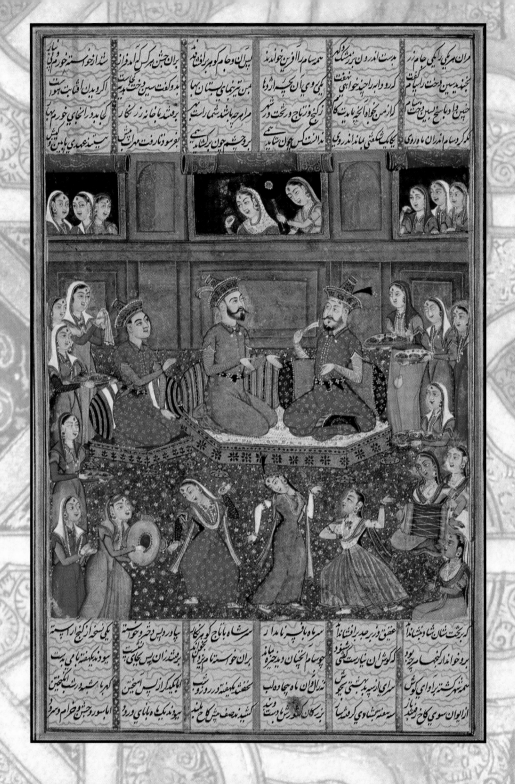

The House of Wisdom

Al-Mamun established a great learning center called the House of **Wisdom**. It had an enormous library filled with **manuscripts** from ancient Greece and other places. Many Arab scientists and **mathematicians** worked together at the House of Wisdom, **translating** the manuscripts into Arabic. They began with the math manuscripts, since they believed that there could be no science without math.

Inspired by the ideas they found in the manuscripts and by talking with each other, the scientists and mathematicians began to write their own books on math. Some of them wrote books about finger counting, which was an ancient way to make **calculations**. Many different forms of finger counting existed, but the one the Arabs used came from ancient Egypt. By 830 A.D., it had been around for more than 3,000 years. Using this system, it was possible to show numbers from 1 through 9,999 with nothing but your fingers!

This picture shows numbers 1 through 9 in the finger-counting method used in Baghdad. The signs for 1, 2, and 3 and those for 7, 8, and 9 look very similar. However, the fingers were positioned lower on the hand when making the numbers 7, 8, and 9. These numbers, as well as all numbers up to 99, were shown with the right hand. The left hand was used to show hundreds and thousands.

Finger counting was a useful system that had advantages. You did not need something to write on or something to write with. You did not even need to know how to write.

Finger counting also had disadvantages. Since you were not writing anything down, you had only your fingers and your brain to keep track of your calculations. Addition and subtraction were not too hard to do, but multiplication and division were difficult.

Scientists and mathematicians at the House of Wisdom realized that a system invented by **Hindu** mathematicians in India had many advantages over finger counting and other math systems. Several centuries before al-Mamun established the House of Wisdom, Hindu mathematicians had invented a place-value number system and a special set of **numerals**. These Hindu inventions provided an easy, clear way to write numbers and made it much easier to solve math problems. In fact, the Hindu numerals and place-value system worked so well that we still use them today!

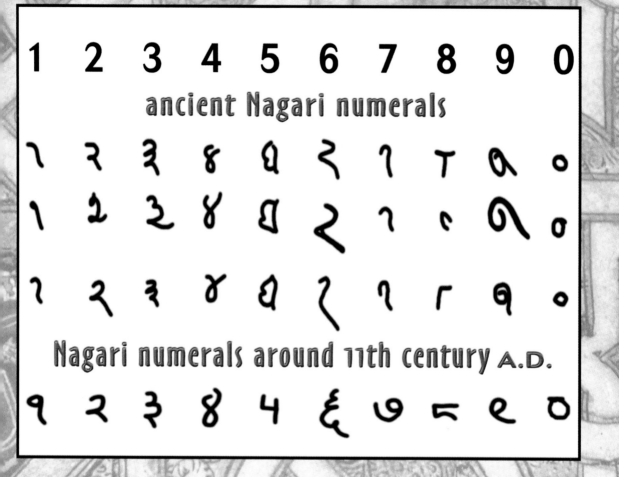

1 2 3 4 5 6 7 8 9 0

ancient Nagari numerals

Nagari numerals around 11th century A.D.

The Hindu numerals shown here were used in different parts of India between the 7th century A.D. and the 11th century A.D. Nagari numerals were considered the most beautiful form of ancient Hindu numerals.

13

Al-Khwarizmi Invents Algebra

The most famous mathematician at the House of Wisdom was a man named al-Khwarizmi (al–hwar-REEZ-me). Around 825 A.D., al-Khwarizmi wrote the first book in Arabic to explain the Hindu number system. This book was titled *Al-Khwarizmi on the Hindu Art of Calculating*. It helped to spread knowledge of the Hindu system and its advantages throughout the Arab world.

Around 830 A.D., al-Khwarizmi wrote another important math book in which he actually invented a completely new kind of math! This math came to be called "algebra" after one of the words in the book's title: "*al-jabr.*" This was the Arabic name of one of the math operations al-Khwarizmi used in the book, and it means "completion."

At the beginning of his algebra book, al-Khwarizmi explained that he invented this new kind of math to help merchants, engineers, and ordinary people with the everyday math problems they had to solve.

The importance of math in the Islamic world shows in its art. The pure beauty of numbers is reflected in the patterns that fill Islamic art. The patterns shown here are from a painting in an Islamic manuscript.

Later Arab and Muslim Mathematicians

The story of algebra didn't end in 830 A.D. Many later Arab and **Muslim** mathematicians made their own contributions.

Al-Khwarizmi died around 850 A.D. That same year, an Arab mathematician named Abu Kamil (ah-BOO kah-MEEL) was born. In an algebra book he wrote around 900 A.D., Abu Kamil praised al-Khwarizmi as the man who "invented all the principles" of algebra. Abu Kamil's book helped to introduce Europeans to algebra about 300 years after he wrote it.

Around 1000 A.D., a great Muslim doctor and scientist named ibn Sina (EE-ben see-NAH) began work on an immense, four-part book titled *The Book of Healing*. One part deals with math, including algebra. We may think it's strange to include math in a book about healing, but Arab and Muslim scientists believed that math was the basis of all science. For them, it was natural to include a section on math in any book about science.

This picture from an ancient Arabic manuscript shows ibn Sina teaching a group of students.

Algebra Finally Reaches Europe

An Italian named Fibonacci (fih-buh-NAH-chee) introduced algebra and the Hindu-Arabic number system into Europe with a book he wrote in 1202, titled the *Book of the **Abacus***. Fibonacci was born in Italy around 1170. He grew up in North Africa, where his father was an Italian government official who oversaw matters of trade. Fibonacci received his education in North Africa from men trained in algebra and the Hindu-Arabic system. As a young man, Fibonacci traveled widely and read many math books, including the one by Abu Kamil.

Like al-Khwarizmi almost 400 years earlier, Fibonacci meant for his book to help merchants with the kind of problems they dealt with every day. He included sample problems dealing with the price of goods, how to calculate profits, and how to convert between the kinds of money used by different countries.

Fibonacci learned much about math and counting systems from the many merchants he met during his travels.

Math for Merchants

Imagine that you are a cloth merchant living in Baghdad in 830 A.D., when algebra is just being invented. You sell beautiful cloth to the wealthy and important people in the city. Every day you have to use math. You have to figure out how much cloth to order and how much it will cost you. Then you have to calculate the price you will charge your **customers** for the cloth. When someone buys cloth, you have to figure out the total price based on how much cloth they bought.

Most merchants use finger counting to make their calculations. However, you want to find a method that will allow you to make your calculations more quickly and easily. You've heard about algebra, the new type of math invented by al-Khwarizmi, and you realize it's just what you've been looking for. On the next few pages, we'll see how algebra can help you solve the math problems you deal with every day.

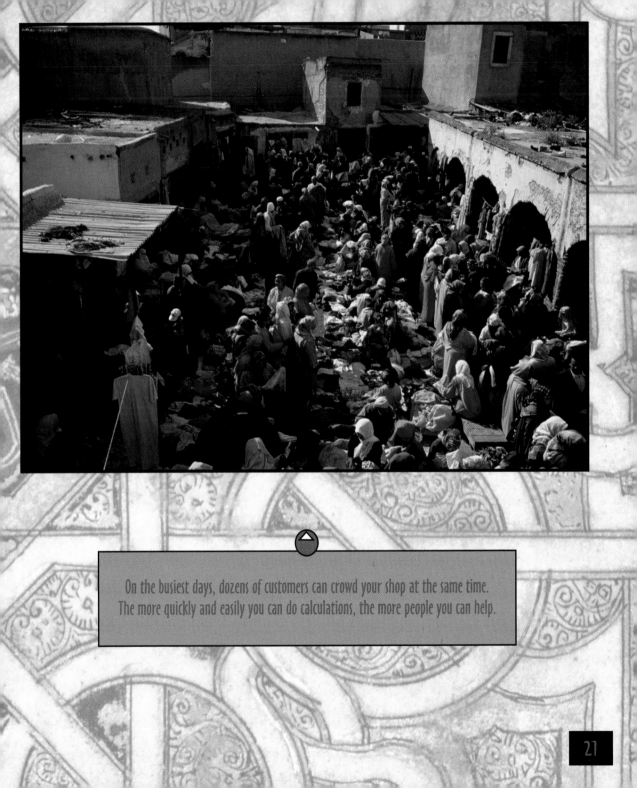

On the busiest days, dozens of customers can crowd your shop at the same time. The more quickly and easily you can do calculations, the more people you can help.

Problem 1:

The cloth seller shows you some new kinds of cloth. He tells you that the blue cloth you bought last month costs $3.00 more per yard than the new green cloth you want to buy today. You paid $7.00 per yard for the blue cloth. How much does the new green cloth cost?

This problem may seem pretty confusing when it's presented as a word problem. When you write it as an algebra equation, however, it seems much simpler and clearer.

The cost of the new green cloth is the unknown amount that you want to find, so it is the variable x in the equation. Adding $3.00 to x equals $7.00, the amount you paid for the blue cloth. Here's how you would write the problem.

$$x \text{ (cost of new green cloth)} + \$3.00 = \$7.00 \text{ (cost of blue cloth)}$$

Now let's go through the steps to solve the problem. You must subtract $3.00 from both sides of the equation.

$$x + \$3.00 - \$3.00 = \$7.00 - \$3.00 = \$4.00$$
$$x = \mathbf{\$4.00}$$
The new green cloth costs $4.00 per yard.

A cloth merchant in Baghdad in 830 A.D. might have sold rolls of cloth
in bright colors and with beautiful patterns similar to the
rolls of cloth shown here.

Problem 2:

The cloth seller shows you the most beautiful red silk you have ever seen. You want al-Mamun, the ruler of the empire, to buy as much of this silk as you can get. The cloth seller tells you that the red silk costs 3 times as much as the yellow silk you've always bought. You pay $8.00 per yard for the yellow silk. How much does the red silk cost?

The first step is to write the problem as an algebra equation. In this equation, the variable x will stand for the cost of the red silk.

$$x \text{ (cost of new red silk)} = 3 \times \$8.00 \text{ (cost of yellow silk)}$$

Multiplying $8.00 by 3 will give you the cost of the red silk.

$$x = 3 \times \$8.00$$
$$x = \$24.00$$

The cost of the red silk is $24.00 per yard.

Wealthy customers often wanted beautiful and expensive cloth that came from distant places, such as silk from China. Silk and other expensive materials were carried from China to the Middle East and Europe in caravans like the one shown here.

Problem 3:

You decide to buy all the red silk that the cloth seller has. He has only 10 yards with him, but that will be enough to show al-Mamun how beautiful the silk is. How much do you have to pay the cloth seller for all his red silk? Remember to start by writing the problem as an algebra equation, with the variable x representing the amount you must pay the cloth seller for all the red silk.

$$x = 10 \times \$24.00$$
$$x = \mathbf{\$240.00}$$

You must pay the cloth seller $240.00 for the 10 yards of red silk.

Problem 4:

Two of your best customers want you to order yellow and purple cloth to decorate their new palace. For the room where they receive guests, they want 4 times as much purple cloth as yellow cloth. You take measurements of the room, then together you and your customers decide that they need 30 yards of yellow cloth. How much purple cloth do they need?

Write the problem as an algebra equation. What will the variable x stand for in this equation?

x (number of yards of purple cloth) $= 4 \times 30$ (number of yards of yellow cloth)

Now complete the multiplication to find the value for x.

$$x = 4 \times 30$$
$$x = 120$$

Your customers will need 120 yards of purple cloth.

Problem 5:

Your customers decide they want an additional 12 yards of purple cloth for their bedroom. How many total yards of purple cloth do they need? You can find the answer with a simple algebra equation. The total number of yards of purple cloth needed, x, equals the sum of the numbers of yards needed for each room.

$$x = 120 + 12$$
$$x = \textbf{132}$$

Your customers need a total of 132 yards of purple cloth for the 2 rooms.

Problem 6:

After seeing the way these customers have decorated their rooms with yellow and purple cloth, their neighbors decide they want to do the same thing using different colors. They decide on gold and blue cloth. They want as many yards of blue cloth as their neighbors ordered of yellow cloth and as many yards of gold cloth as the neighbors ordered of purple. They also want an additional 12 yards of gold cloth for their bedroom. How many yards of gold cloth do you need to order for your new customers?

Since the new customers want exactly the same amount of cloth as your original customers ordered, only in different colors, you can use the same equations you used on pages 26 and 27 to find how many yards of gold cloth to order. As before, x equals the number of yards needed for the room where guests are received in the first equation.

The painting on page 29 gives us an idea of what a palace bedroom might have looked like. It comes from a book written around 1410.

$$x = 4 \times 30$$
$$x = \mathbf{120}$$

You need to order 120 yards of gold cloth for your new customers to use in the room where they receive guests.

In the second equation, x equals the total number of yards needed for both rooms.

$$x = 120 + 12$$
$$x = \mathbf{132}$$

You need to order a total of 132 yards of gold cloth for the 2 rooms the new customers want to decorate.

Problem 7:

For the final problem, let's see what the equation would look like if you put both equations in problem 6 into a single equation. This single equation will combine the two operations that were covered separately before. Keep in mind that the parentheses in this equation tell you which operation to perform first. They tell you to multiply 30 by 4 before you add 12. What does x stand for in this new equation?

$$x = (4 \times 30) + 12$$

$$x = 120 + 12$$

$$x = \mathbf{132} \ (132 \text{ yards of gold cloth})$$

Whenever you work on algebra problems, remember that algebra was invented to help people solve practical problems. It's not the only way to solve the problems, but it's often simpler and clearer than other methods. Now that you know something about algebra, see if you can find ways that it can help you solve math problems you face every day!

Glossary

abacus (AA-buh-kuhs) A tool for making calculations.

calculation (kal-kyuh-LAY-shun) The act of solving math problems.

constant (KAHN-stunt) The name given to numbers in algebra problems, since they do not change.

customer (KUHS-tuh-muhr) Someone who buys goods or services.

equation (ih-KWAY-zhun) A statement that two numbers are equal.

Hindu (HIN-doo) Someone who practices the faith of Hinduism.

Islamic (is-LAH-mik) Having to do with the faith of Islam.

manuscript (MAN-yuh-skript) A book written entirely by hand.

mathematician (math-muh-TIH-shun) Someone who is an authority on math.

Muslim (MUHZ-luhm) Someone who practices the faith of Islam.

numeral (NOO-muh-ruhl) A sign that stands for a number.

translate (TRANS-layt) To take something written in one language and write it in another language.

variable (VAIR-ee-uh-buhl) A sign in algebra problems that stands for any one of many possible numbers.

wisdom (WIZ-duhm) Knowledge and good judgement based on experience.

Index